UNCOMMON FAVOR
STUDY JOURNAL

AN INTERACTIVE RESOURCE FOR INDIVIDUALS AND SMALL GROUPS

HEATHER JOHNSTON

Copyright © 2022 by Heather Johnston

All rights reserved. No part of this publication may be reproduced, distributed, or transmitted in any form or by any means, including photocopying, recording, or other electronic or mechanical methods, without the prior written permission of the publisher, except in the case of brief quotations embodied in critical reviews and certain other noncommercial uses permitted by copyright law. For permission requests, write to the publisher at the address below.

Fedd Books
P.O. Box 341973
Austin, TX 78734

www.thefeddagency.com

Published in association with The Fedd Agency, Inc., a literary agency.

All Scripture quotations, unless otherwise indicated, are taken from the Holy Bible, New International Version®, NIV®. Copyright ©1973, 1978, 1984, 2011 by Biblica, Inc.™ Used by permission of Zondervan. All rights reserved worldwide. www.zondervan.com The "NIV" and "New International Version" are trademarks registered in the United States Patent and Trademark Office by Biblica, Inc.™

Scripture quotations marked (NASB) have been taken from the (NASB®) New American Standard Bible®, Copyright © 1960, 1971, 1977, 1995, 2020 by The Lockman Foundation. Used by permission. All rights reserved. www.lockman.org.

Scripture quotations marked (NKJV) have been taken from the New King James Version®. Copyright © 1982 by Thomas Nelson. Used by permission. All rights reserved.

Design by Deryn Pieterse

ISBN: 978-1-949784-77-0

eISBN: 978-1-949784-78-7

Library of Congress Number: 2021910930

Printed in the United States of America

First Edition 22 23 24 25 /6 5 4 3 2

CONTENTS

INTRODUCTION v

CHAPTER 1: CHUTZPAH 1

CHAPTER 2: CHOSEN AND DISTINGUISHED 9

CHAPTER 3: BECOMING A TALMID 19

CHAPTER 4: HIS YOKE IS EASY 29

CHAPTER 5: A TOWEL 35

CHAPTER 6: LECH LECHAH: GO YOU 43

CHAPTER 7: TOGETHER 51

CHAPTER 8: FINDING HOME 59

CHAPTER 9: SOLITUDE, SILENCE, AND LISTENING 65

CHAPTER 10: TRUE AUTHORITY 75

CHAPTER 11: OVERCOMING EVIL 83

CHAPTER 12: ADVANCING 93

ENDNOTES 105

SMALL GROUP LEADER GUIDE 107

ADDITIONAL RESOURCES 110

INTRODUCTION

The woman was not welcome at the dinner party, but she came anyway. In fact, not only was she not invited, but she also pushed her way through the crowd toward the guest of honor—an action both scandalous and shocking. And once she had the guest of honor's attention, she brought all the dinnertime conversation to a halt with an audacious gesture—she poured oil on His feet. Other guests watched in horror, some even letting out scathing remarks.

Was this a scene from reality television? A YouTube clip? Actually, it was neither. The scene took place in the home of a wealthy Pharisee in ancient Judea more than two thousand years ago. The woman was Mary of Bethany—Lazarus's sister and a "woman … who lived a sinful life" (Luke 7:37) and was radically changed by God's mercy. A woman who was permanently marked and transformed by the compassion of a local rabbi named Jesus.

Mary's audacious gesture was an act of utter worship at the feet of her rabbi. After her extravagant and slightly inappropriate act, there's a plot twist of an ending. Rather than rebuking Mary for interrupting the meal and wasting her valuable perfume, Jesus said, "When she poured this perfume on my body, she did it to prepare me for burial" (Matthew 26:12).

This is unapologetic, glorious *chutzpah*—in Hebrew, "raw nerve driven by passion."

Can you relate to Mary? Frankly, many of us probably relate more to Judas's reaction when he rebuked Mary and questioned why she didn't just sell the perfume so the money could be given to the poor. You've got a thousand dollars' worth of perfume in your hand—pour it on a guy's feet and apply it with your hair, or sell it for charity? (Yet, we learn that sometimes being sensible leads us nowhere.)

This story begs the question: What does it truly mean to be a disciple of Jesus today? Are we too safe in our faith? In our prayers? Do we dream too small? These are the questions that compelled me to write *Uncommon Favor*, the book on which this study journal is based. In fact, I believe we need a radical review of what it means to be a *talmid*—a disciple of Jesus. By that, I am not talking about a new theology. Just the opposite. I am talking about a return to the biblical roots of what it means to be a follower of Jesus who intimately and passionately pursues His purposes in their life.

To be clear, this is not a Bible study. Rather, the purpose of this resource is to help you embark on a personal journey toward becoming a fully surrendered and committed disciple of Jesus. Like Mary of Bethany.

The invitation is there. Jesus is calling all of us to more. Like any journey into the unknown, this process will not be straightforward, ordinary, or safe. It is an invitation to live beyond predictable faith, where Jesus will meet you personally with love and fire in His eyes. And I guarantee this: the journey will not disappoint. It may be painful and disruptive—and it may shake the dust off your controlled, safe life—but it will bring joy, intimacy, and a deeper relationship with your Father than you could have ever imagined.

Indeed, the life of a true disciple involves a risk-taking relationship with Him. In this partnership, one moves through the human dilemma of helplessness into a wholehearted response to the Holy Spirit that gives the disciple power to influence their world. This is not about you; it was never about you. What a joyous, startling relief!

I have written this study journal for those who have been walking with God for a while as well as for those who are just beginning a serious relationship with Him. You will engage in a decision-making process not unlike what a first-century talmid, or disciple, might have experienced.

As you set out on this transformational path, you will explore new territory within yourself in solitude with God. Our relationship with Him does not at first unite us with others; it separates us. He separates us before He makes us whole. Our uniqueness and identity are wrapped up in the reality of His personal love for us, and this study journal draws you into that understanding and way of thinking. You will need to intentionally set aside time to meet with Him as you embark on this journey. You will find this encounter to be both holy and illuminating.

The twelve lessons mirror the content of each respective chapter in the main book. The intent is for this study journal to act as a gateway through which you can more thoroughly explore the rich landscape of *Uncommon Favor*. In keeping with the life of a first-century talmid of Jesus, each lesson is made up of six tools you will need to take your journey.

PATHWAY: this represents the main point or theme, the destination toward which the chapter will direct you.

LANDMARKS: these are the main truths and goals we want to pursue along the way.

KEY: the Bible verse that is central to unlocking that chapter's truths.

JOURNEY: this provides the necessary tools needed to "walk out" the chapter.

PRAYER: to bring what you have learned from the lesson before the Father.

DESTINATION: wraps up the end of each chapter and provides the takeaways needed to incorporate the lesson into your daily journey as a talmid.

This study journal may also be used by small groups. Once you have gone through the personal process in each chapter, you can meet in a small group to talk through some of your decisions and discoveries. This step is also vital as it will lead to discussions about how to influence your world. There are some helpful suggestions for small group leaders at the back of this study journal.

I'm excited to take part in this journey with you. The greatest privilege on this earth is to be a beloved son or daughter of the Most High King, and my prayer is that this study journal will help you grow closer to Him in ways you never thought possible!

CHAPTER 1

CHUTZPAH

Getting our prayers answered doesn't result from timid and polite appeals. Rather, it comes from the deep conviction that we are esteemed children in God's house and that our Father will give us what we ask.

—Uncommon Favor

PATHWAY

The main point of this chapter is to understand what it means to cultivate a spiritual life filled with chutzpah and to grow in the confidence that God delights in responding to our needs.

LANDMARKS

- Whatever season of life you are in, chutzpah is the agent that will bring change. If we stay where we are—where we are comfortable and safe—we will slowly fossilize and die there.

- God gives without measure to the one who is certain that their request will be granted. This does not mean we escape hardships, but it does give us a mindset of confidence and tenacity.

- A talmid with chutzpah respectfully acknowledges their own shortcomings and deficiencies while seizing upon the transformational truth that God not only loves them but also knows and likes them. True faith focuses on what God is like.

KEY

Then Jesus said to them, "Suppose you have a friend, and you go to him at midnight and say, 'Friend, lend me three loaves of bread; a friend of mine on a journey has come to me, and I have no food to offer him.' And suppose the one inside answers, 'Don't bother me. The door is already locked, and my children and I are in bed. I can't get up and give you anything.' I tell you, even though he will not get up and give you the bread because of friendship, yet because of your shameless audacity he will surely get up and give you as much as you need." —Luke 11:5-8

JOURNEY

THE GIFT OF DISRUPTION

We see reflected in this parable that the journey toward chutzpah begins with a disruption. That disruption may arrive in the form of an unannounced friend coming to stay with you, or unexpectedly being laid off from your job, or God provoking you to discontentment with your life. While disruptions often come unwelcomed, they can be gifts that shake us awake. Jesus' original *talmidim* (disciples) were blessed with the gift of disruption. They all faced a moment when they had to drop their nets and walk away from their former lives. Disruption leads us into a new experience. To truly be Jesus' disciples, we undergo a dramatic turning toward Him and away from all else. Change and disruption prepare us for new horizons but only if we move forward and seize new opportunities.

1. What's the biggest disruption you've experienced in life? How did you feel during that experience? What would it look like for you to begin to view such disruptions as opportunities rather than setbacks?

HOLY DESPERATION

In most cases, a holy disruption will lead us into desperation. As seen in the parable of the persistent neighbor, when the man was disrupted by his surprise guest, he became desperate for more food. For many, an unwelcome disruption in our lives can be the catalyst to move us toward a desperation for more of God. It seems that there is a certain holy desperation necessary for chutzpah to arise from the human spirit and for change to occur within our lives. When the desperation comes, God then has an invitation to invade our lives and bring about a breakthrough. We often don't even know we need this breakthrough. But in the place of desperation, we suddenly see that we are weak and vulnerable and desperately need God to come into our lives.

2. Have you ever experienced a disruption that led you to a place of extreme desperation for God? Do you want to come to a place where you invite God in to change your life? What stands in the way of holy desperation for you?

RAW NERVE

If disruptions produce desperation, then desperation produces chutzpah. Chutzpah is the spiritual essence of an aggressive and passionate faith. In other words, chutzpah is raw nerve. In Luke 11, the man banged on his neighbor's door with unapologetic audacity. Chutzpah is not about persistence in prayer but insistence that God answer our prayers, because we are certain He hears us and delights to answer. Without intensity and shameless courage, our personal life with God is shallow and inauthentic.

3. How well do you relate to the neighbor who boldly asked for bread from his friend? Do you share his faith-filled boldness in your relationship with God? Why or why not? In what ways do you think your spiritual chutzpah could be strengthened? What would be required of you? What is one thing that hinders you from embracing a deeper life with God (habits, addictions, busyness, etc.)?

4. Is there a specific prayer you have been asking God to answer? Are you in need of a breakthrough in a certain area of your life? If so, what is it? How would your prayer life look different if you began to pray from a place of boldness and insistence that God answer? Write out this chutzpah prayer.

EXTREME FAMILIARITY

Chutzpah feels brazen and inappropriate. How dare we approach the God of the universe and insist that He answer our prayer. But extreme familiarity is the critical point Jesus made in the parable in Luke. The man knew his friend would answer the door and give him what he needed. Only if God is truly our Father do we dare approach Him in this manner. A daughter or son can make requests of their father that no one else can make, based on their intimate relationship with him as the one who is loving, protecting, and providing. Earnestness deepens our understanding of God and enables us to possess an intimate life of faith for ourselves.

5. What emotions do you experience when you think about asking God to answer prayers centered around your personal needs or desires? Do you feel embarrassed, selfish, uncomfortable, or guilty? Why or why not? How would your life change if you began to approach Him as a daughter or son who believes He will give you good gifts?

Jesus was clear in Luke 11:9–10 when He said:

> So I say to you: Ask and it will be given to you; seek and you will find; knock and the door will be opened to you. For everyone who asks receives; the one who seeks finds; and to the one who knocks, the door will be opened.

We can take this as a promise from God. He will answer our prayers.

PRAYER

God, I thank You that You are my Father. You have called me into an intimate relationship with You. I pray that You will help me see every disruption in my life as a divine intervention from You. Help me respond to these disruptions as opportunities and lead me into that holy desperation for more of You. There are areas of my life that need breakthrough. There are prayers I have prayed for a long time that need to be answered. I boldly and shamelessly come before You now and insist that You answer my prayers. As Your child I know You graciously give good gifts to Your children; You withhold nothing from the ones You love. Increase the chutzpah in my life and give me an aggressive faith to believe You for bigger things! Amen.

DESTINATION

Here are four simple steps to begin walking into a life of chutzpah.

1. Change the wording of your prayers into faith-filled, declarative prayers.

2. Thank God for the work He is already doing, whether you see it yet or not.

3. Ask from the position of a child of God who is the object of your Father's favor and delight.

4. Write out your requests before the Lord. Now write out some of God's promises associated with fulfilling the desires of our heart. Stay with your requests until you hear Him respond to you.

Chutzpah will lead you into personal transformation. God will respond in a powerful way when you expectantly ask Him to invade your life and take you deeper. This is the foundation for the rest of this journey to becoming a disciple.

CHAPTER 2

CHOSEN AND DISTINGUISHED

When God calls us, He gives us a new identity. He separates us from the status quo and from the worthless things in our lives, and He prepares us to walk in absolute dependency on Him.

—Uncommon Favor

PATHWAY

God invites us to passionately respond to Jesus' unique call on our lives and to boldly follow Him in faith and obedience as He illuminates our purpose.

LANDMARKS

- When God chooses us, He comes and meets our greatest human need: to be singled out, chosen, identified with Him, and summoned to a life of unique purpose.
- God calls us because He loves us, not because He needs us. He calls us as we are, not as we think we should be, and gives us a new, unique identity in Him.
- Bold moves are critical to passion. A talmid discerns the door Jesus is opening and courageously walks through it, even if they do not see a clear path beyond.

KEY

One day as Jesus was standing by the Lake of Gennesaret, the people were crowding around him and listening to the word of God. He saw at the water's edge two boats, left there by the fishermen, who were washing their nets. He got into one of the boats, the one belonging to Simon, and asked him to put out a little from shore. Then he sat down and taught the people from the boat. When he had finished speaking, he said to Simon, "Put out into deep water, and let down the nets for a catch." Simon answered, "Master, we've worked hard all night and haven't caught anything. But because you say so, I will let down the nets." When they had done so, they caught such a large number of fish that their nets began to break. So they signaled their partners in the other boat to come and help them, and they came and filled both boats so full that they began to sink. When Simon Peter saw this, he fell at Jesus' knees and said, "Go away from me, Lord; I am a sinful man!" For he and all his companions were astonished at the catch of fish they had taken, and so were James and John, the sons of Zebedee, Simon's partners. Then Jesus said to Simon, "Don't be afraid; from now on you will fish for people." So they pulled their boats up on shore, left everything and followed him. —Luke 5:1-11

JOURNEY

Have you ever paused to think, *What is my identity?* If you have, then you probably listed off several roles you play—spouse, parent, co-worker, student, child, friend. Maybe you thought about some of your defining accomplishments or some of your failures. This world and its culture impose a laundry list of identities on us. It is easy to identify ourselves in the context of what others think.

Invite the Holy Spirit to lead you through this prayer and exercise.

God, I invite You in to help shine light on how I view myself and my identity. Show me clearly how I have defined myself. It's hard for me to see myself apart from the labels I've acquired in life and the expectations of a culture that tries to press me into its mold. Help me see the truth of how I view myself. Amen.

1. How would you describe yourself? Is how you view yourself based on how others view you? Have you put your worth and identity in your accomplishments? In what ways? How might you let deep failures define you?

2. We can sometimes assume false identities. This might look like believing a lie that has been spoken over you. For example, if you grew up with a parent who told you that you would not amount to anything, you have likely lived your life from that place. Or perhaps you made a bad business decision that cost you and others a significant amount of money, and now you live with that failure. Maybe you have a child who has gone down a bad path, and you have taken on the identity of a failed parent. What false identities have you allowed yourself to believe?

Jesus came onto the scene in the first century with a unique mission: to call His people into an intimate relationship with Him, to give them a new identity through His love, and to partner with them to make disciples. He knew the greatest human need is to feel individually seen and known—to have a unique identity.

We see the approach Jesus took in calling His original disciples in Luke 5:1–11. Though two thousand years have passed, it is the same rhythm or "calling pattern" Jesus uses today to call His talmidim.

JESUS COMES INTO OUR LIVES WITH POWER

In verses 4–6, we see an awesome display of Jesus' power:

> When he had finished speaking, he said to Simon, "Put out into deep water, and let down the nets for a catch." Simon answered, "Master, we've worked hard all night and haven't caught anything. But because you say so, I will let down the nets." When they had done so, they caught such a large number of fish that their nets began to break.

Jesus comes into our lives in an undeniable way. He makes Himself known to us so we can recognize His call to step into the new identity He wants to give us.

3. How have you seen God's hand leading, guiding, and working in your life? In what ways has Jesus made Himself known to you? How has He led you to make certain decisions?

JESUS QUALIFIES US

In verses 8–9, we witness Peter's very human response to Jesus' power.

> When Simon Peter saw this, he fell at Jesus' knees and said, "Go away from me, Lord; I am a sinful man!" For he and all his companions were astonished at the catch of fish they had taken.

He could not believe such a powerful God would want to partner with him, a sinful man. When Jesus calls us into His life of power to be disciples, we don't feel like worthy candidates. But He sees who we are becoming and loves us as we are now. His love alone is the benchmark that qualifies us to be disciples.

4. How have you responded like Peter to God's call on your life? What makes it hard for you to believe like Peter that God wants to trust you and to partner with you in His purposes?

JESUS GIVES US A NEW IDENTITY

We see Jesus' response to Peter in verse 10. Essentially, He told Peter, "Don't be afraid of this call on your life. You will help prepare disciples for me. This is your assignment. You are no longer going to be a fisherman; I am giving you a brand-new identity." When Jesus chooses us, He comes and meets our great human need: to be singled out, identified with Him, and summoned. Jesus wants to distinguish you and to give you a new identity.

Ask the Holy Spirit to guide you in this prayer, and then respond to the following questions.

God, I declare that You alone are the giver of my identity and that who I am is only discovered in the context of Your perfect love for me. Show me at this very moment how You are calling me out and distinguishing me. I ask that You use today as a defining moment to express Your powerful love for me. Jesus, how do You want me to partner with You? I want to be used by You to impact others. I reject any false identities I have allowed myself to believe. What is the new identity You want to give me? Amen.

5. How is Jesus uniquely distinguishing you? What is He saying about your new identity? What do you see that needs to change moving forward?

JESUS CALLS US TO HAVE BOLDNESS FOR THE MISSION

Once Peter understood that He was chosen and distinguished, he moved from a place of helplessness to a place of hopefulness and action. Peter's immediate response to his new identity was to leave everything and follow Jesus (see v. 11). A new identity and a burning heart for God are not enough; we take steps to boldly follow Him. And He often asks us for that boldness when we don't even know the next step, let alone what the future will hold.

PRAYER

Jesus, I recognize that You have called me out and asked me to follow You in obedience. I have no idea what this journey will bring, but I do know Your love is powerful enough for me to drop everything, to believe I am forgiven and follow You. Give me courage and boldness to take the steps You ask me to take. Lead me out of where I have been with Your mighty love for me. Show me how to take the next steps of faith. Amen.

DESTINATION

Here are some steps you can take to respond to Jesus' unique call to boldly follow Him in faith and obedience.

1. It takes daily discipline to be a talmid of Jesus. Examine your habits and daily rhythms. What is Jesus saying to you about your present lifestyle? Responding to Jesus' call is an inside-out job. What do you need to change from the inside to better position yourself as a talmid?

2. Attune your ear to hear His voice as you sit at His feet in prayer. Identify what God is showing you to be worthless in your life as well as where your efforts have come up empty or clearly have been reduced. What do you believe He wants from you?

3. On a practical level, what would it look like for you to drop your former thinking and way of life to follow Him closely? Write down the top three or four things you need to eliminate in your life or thinking to cultivate deeper intimacy with Him.

4. Do you have any sense of where Jesus may be leading you? Consider asking Him to open the doors that are uniquely intended for you.

Peter had no idea what it would mean to follow Rabbi Jesus. Yet, the encounter with Jesus was so deeply revealing, holy, and life-altering that it transformed Peter. Jesus not only distinguished Peter, but He also gave Peter the power to leave his sinful life and take on a new identity. Peter dropped his net, which represented to him a former life. Then he followed Jesus and joined His mission. When you understand that King Jesus has singled you out and chosen you, it will forever alter your life too.

CHAPTER 3

BECOMING A TALMID

The talmid's aim wasn't just to learn from the teacher but to become like him. The talmid was devoted to everything the rabbi said and did. The rabbi helped the talmid discover who they were and how they fit into a larger picture.

—Uncommon Favor

PATHWAY

In the first two chapters, we explored the vital elements one must have to become a talmid: the need for chutzpah and the understanding that we are chosen and distinguished by Jesus. It's now time to step into the journey of a talmid by surrendering ourselves to follow and become like Rabbi Jesus.

LANDMARKS

- Jesus honored many of the Jewish religious traditions of His day, including the structure for preparing disciples, or talmidim. He implemented this structure when He chose His own talmidim.

- A talmid makes the decision to place Jesus above people, pursuits, and possessions.

- A talmid counts the cost of becoming a disciple of Jesus and takes a radical inventory of their commitment. A talmid asks, "Am I ready to put Jesus above everything in my life?"

KEY

Large crowds were traveling with Jesus, and turning to them he said: "If anyone comes to me and does not hate father and mother, wife and children, brothers and sisters—yes, even their own life—such a person cannot be my disciple. And whoever does not carry their cross and follow me cannot be my disciple. "Suppose one of you wants to build a tower. Won't you first sit down and estimate the cost to see if you have enough money to complete it? For if you lay the foundation and are not able to finish it, everyone who sees it will ridicule you, saying, 'This person began to build and wasn't able to finish.' "Or suppose a king is about to go to war against another king. Won't he first sit down and consider whether he is able with ten thousand men to oppose the one coming against him with twenty thousand? If he is not able, he will send a delegation while the other is still a long way off and will ask for terms of peace. In the same way, those of you who do not give up everything you have cannot be my disciples." —Luke 14:25-33

JOURNEY

We cannot attempt to follow Jesus through the context of our modern culture. Rather, it is far better to enter into the first-century paradigm, into the process of a talmid choosing a rabbi. The power of following Jesus actually lies in understanding the impact of this choice. People living within the Jewish culture at this time knew a relationship between a rabbi and a talmid was intensely personal and life changing. It required talmidim to give up their personal preferences to become like their rabbi.

It can feel daunting, maybe even unfathomable, to follow Jesus so closely that you would become like Him. We may believe we daily fail to exude even a shred of godliness in our lives. We ask, "How can I possibly emulate Jesus?"

It is only when we begin to open our shaky hands and examine the things we hold so tightly that the Holy Spirit exposes those areas we have given preeminence above God.

Like the first-century disciples, we cannot follow Rabbi Jesus without first making three important exchanges. Our devotion to become like Him supersedes our love for anything or anyone else. So God lovingly leads us into the necessary surrender of:

1. people
2. pursuits
3. possessions

The following exercise is a serious undertaking in the journey of a disciple. Look for a few hours of solitude to go through this process. Turn off your cell phone; find a babysitter; leave your laptop behind; and tell your loved ones you will be off the grid for a while. It is essential that you get alone with God in a comfortable and quiet location to undertake this exercise.

Many people were eager to follow Rabbi Jesus. They traveled from town to town with Him, listened to His teachings, and experienced His miracles. But Jesus made a qualifying statement that His way is not for everyone. He challenged the masses to stop and seriously consider the cost of following Him.

JESUS BEFORE PEOPLE

Jesus addresses our intimate relationships. To follow Jesus, a talmid is willing to lay down the people in their life to pursue Him.

1. Who are the most important people in your life? A child, a spouse, a friend, or a dating relationship? Would you say you hold on to any of these loved ones too tightly? Do you tend to put any of your loved ones and their opinions of you before God in your life? In what ways?

2. Sometimes, our value for relationships can cause us to fear others' opinions, which keeps us from following Jesus and doing what He asks of us. Would you be willing to follow Jesus even if it affects or separates you from some of your closest relationships? What would that look like? How would you explain your actions?

Consider using this prayer to surrender the significant people in your life to God.

I recognize that I hold too tightly to these people in my life [name them]. *I realize that I have given them first place before You. I now give them to You, God, in exchange for Your life and power to be the foremost thing. I trust that You will take care of my people and my relationships. I also give up their opinions of me in exchange for Your opinion of me. Help me not to fear others so I can follow You more intimately. Amen.*

JESUS BEFORE PURSUITS

In Luke 14:26 Jesus addresses our pursuits. Jesus knows we are prone to idolize success and hold tightly to what we envision for our future. This was as true in the first century as it is now. A first-century talmid was willing to surrender every aspect of their life to follow their rabbi: their family, career, dreams, expectations, and resources. Why would Jesus ask us for anything less?

3. **Think about your future. What do you envision? Is it a high-profile career with accolades and prestige? Is it a spouse and a family with a white picket fence? A life as a missionary in a foreign country or as a well-known author? A lucrative business and wealthy inheritance for your family and others? While none of these things are inherently wrong or bad, be honest with yourself. Do you hold too tightly to your ideal future? Our thoughts reveal our idols. And what we idolize determines where we invest our time, talent, and treasure. Dreams are not naturally bad or wrong. God plants dreams in our heart. However, if you have placed your dream above God's will, then it is time to reevaluate your priorities.**

4. What would it look like for you to surrender your pursuits to God? What do you think God would want to do with your life if you gave Him an unconditional yes? What scares you about yielding your dreams to Him? Lean into this fear of relinquishing your dreams. Make a list of the things you dream of, and then think and pray about your list. What items honor God, and as you pursue them, will lead you deeper into the surrendered life in Christ? Which items will not?

5. Look at the list you made and now make a second list. This time, name only items you are willing to surrender to God right now. Be honest with yourself; this is between you and God. Don't include anything on your list that you aren't ready to willingly surrender.

6. Now make a third list—your "not yet" list. These are the things you are not ready to surrender. You will want to keep this list handy. Pull it out on a regular basis and pray about it. God is doing a good work in you and already knows your heart—this kind of honesty is both freeing and critical to living as a fully committed talmid. Know that as you surrender your "not yet" list to Him, He has the ability and desire to woo you deeper into His love. It may be only a matter of time before you find yourself moving some of your "not yet" items to the second list! This is a process.

God, thank You for the dreams You have placed in my heart. I know that oftentimes You can work through our dreams, but I don't want any of the dreams in my heart to be above Your timing and Your plans. Forgive me for placing them above You. God, I have had plenty of time to envision my future, and now I surrender it to You. I cannot improve upon Your plans for my life. I give You my unconditional yes. I will go wherever You lead me, and I will do whatever You ask me to do. I just want to be used by You to change the world. I step across a threshold today into Your much grander plans for my life. Amen.

JESUS BEFORE POSSESSIONS

Jesus also addresses the area of finances and possessions. In Luke 14:33 He says we cannot be His disciples if we do not give up everything we have. Another translation says it this way: "Whoever of you does not forsake all that he has cannot be My disciple" (NKJV). Jesus knew how wealth and materialism tempt His people.

7. In what areas of your life have you recognized a love and longing for material possessions over God? How has this kept you from pursuing God and His kingdom in a deeper way? How does placing Jesus at the center of everything enable us to loosen all holds that possessions might have on us?

PRAYER

Jesus, forgive me for the ways I have loved money and material possessions above You. Help me see the areas of my life that this affects. God, I yield up all that I am and all that I have to You. I recognize that I am just a steward of Your resources and nothing belongs to me. I exchange the wealth of this world for the wealth of Your kingdom and all that You want me to experience. Amen.

DESTINATION

Giving up control of possessions and money is no small task. Surrendering our most precious people, pursuits, and possessions can feel like the end of our life as we know it. And it is. But God promises that "Whoever has my commands and keeps them is the one who loves me. The one who loves me will be loved by my Father, and I too will love them and show myself to them" (John 14:21).

In this process of surrendering our lives to God, we enter into the experience of a talmid. We have counted the cost and decided Jesus is the rabbi worth following. We are then given the promise of 2 Corinthians 3:18: "But we all, with unveiled faces, looking as in a mirror at the glory of the Lord, are being transformed into the same image from glory to glory" (NASB). In this place of total surrender, we become transformed into His image. As a talmid, we follow our rabbi to the brink of surrender and, miraculously, we become like Him.

CHAPTER 4

HIS YOKE IS EASY

It is easy to see why the disciples left everything to follow Jesus. They were in the presence of holiness. As they left their sinful lives behind to follow Him, they grew near to God and brought heaven to Earth. Jesus' yoke was freedom—not only for themselves but also for others.

—Uncommon Favor

PATHWAY

Jesus invites us into a life that will entail work and sacrifice. However, when we take on Rabbi Jesus' yoke of freedom—as opposed to the world's yoke of burden—we receive the peace of a renewed mind and the power to manifest the kingdom of heaven here on Earth.

LANDMARKS

- In Jesus' time, when a talmid "put on" a rabbi's yoke, it meant that the talmid would emulate their rabbi's way of life. They would follow their rabbi's interpretation and application of the law to everyday living. This yoke was the main consideration for a prospective talmid.

- Jesus' yoke differed from other rabbis in that His way of life was about self-denial and uniquely seeking the success of others—it provided the platform for the inbreaking of the *Malchut Shemayim*, or kingdom of heaven.[1]

- In taking Jesus' yoke, His disciples made a calculated lifelong decision to participate in His redemptive mission to bring heaven to Earth.

KEY

> Come to me, all you who are weary and burdened, and I will give you rest. Take my yoke upon you and learn from me, for I am gentle and humble in heart, and you will find rest for your souls. For my yoke is easy and my burden is light.
> —Matthew 11:28-30

JOURNEY

If you are deep inside Christian culture, then it can feel like rules and obligations dictate your life with Jesus. We try so hard to clean ourselves up, but we ultimately spiral into shame and self-hate when we fall short. Secular culture doesn't have much to provide in this way either. It is easy to look around and be overwhelmed by the world's lack of answers. The world tells us we can be loose and that truth is relative. But if you've experienced that life, then you know it only brings emptiness and anxiety. So where do we turn?

According to Scripture, the human condition in the first century was much like it is now. Jesus came to address this situation. Both the religious rulers and the secular world offered a path to a fulfilled life. And yet, Jesus vehemently warned people to flee from the religious Pharisees who imposed an unattainable and unbearable law; He also told His disciples to sin no more and forsake this world. Jesus saw these pressures from culture and introduced a whole new yoke, a new order, for living—one that would not only fulfill our deep desires but also be multiplied to those around us.

THE YOKE OF A RENEWED MIND

Jesus' famous Sermon on the Mount contains some of His primary teaching and can be referred to as His yoke—or how He interprets the law of God as given under Moses. How many times have you quickly skimmed through these verses without stopping to consider their meaning? These are not merely feel-good verses; they are the first unveiling of Jesus' interpretation of how to live as one of His talmidim. He disclosed a new way of living that is contrary to our natural instincts. It is here that He envisioned a heavenly kingdom of people on Earth who deeply love one another and daily renew their minds regarding what is true.

At first it seems like Jesus' yoke requires an even stricter way of life for His followers than the Pharisees'. But Jesus offered an easier yoke—not based on rules or conduct, but on a pure heart toward others. This is the yoke of a renewed mind.

In Matthew 5–7, Jesus revealed to His talmidim how to daily renew their minds and live in freedom from sin and bondage. Jesus understood that He had entered a broken and hurting world. He knew people could only be set free through a genuine, personal encounter with Him.

1. In what areas of your life do you feel burdened and weighed down? Are you in a seemingly overwhelming financial situation, a recurring addiction to alcohol or sexual impurity, or a hopeless cycle of depression and anxiety? Explain. Where do you need a personal breakthrough with God?

2. Do you believe God wants to have a personal encounter with you? Why or why not? How do you think His power and love would affect your daily life as well as the big problems you are facing? How would Jesus' yoke of peace and a renewed mind change your life?

Take some time to lay your burdens at Jesus' feet and ask Him to take control.

Jesus, I declare that You are powerful enough to set every captive free and to renew my mind. I envision myself bringing all my sin, wounds, and bondage to You and I lay them at Your feet. I turn each one over to You and exchange all my burdens to take on Your yoke of peace. I pray that I will experience the tangible power and freedom that come from living under Your yoke. Thank You for bringing a brand-new yoke and that it is Your desire for me to live under it for a lifetime. I submit my mind to You, and I ask that You daily renew it. Amen.

THE YOKE OF POWER AND FREEDOM

> As you go, proclaim this message: "The kingdom of heaven has come near." Heal the sick, raise the dead, cleanse those who have leprosy, drive out demons. Freely you have received; freely give. —Matthew 10:7–8

Jesus declared that the kingdom of heaven has come! Then He commanded His disciples to go. He said, "freely you have received; freely give." What Jesus means is, "Now that I have set you free from your sin and bondage, you have the responsibility and the power of the Spirit to go replicate My ministry and set other people free from their sin and bondage." As His talmidim, we are also now His ambassadors in this world, doing the same things He did.

3. What would your daily life look like if you began praying heaven down to Earth? How would this change your prayers? What are practical, small steps of boldness you can take to facilitate the kingdom of heaven on Earth?

4. Who in your life needs to be set free from the yoke of bondage and step into Jesus' yoke of peace and freedom? What can you do to help them be released from this bondage? How can you help them find freedom? What will your next steps be?

DESTINATION

Jesus, thank You for personally setting me free from the burden and yoke of this world. I step into the power and freedom of Your yoke, and I ask for boldness to enter the realm where people are hurting and need personal breakthrough in their lives. Please show me opportunities in my day to facilitate the kingdom of heaven on Earth. I recognize that as Your disciple, I am now Your ambassador to a broken world that needs You. Give me the courage to step out of my comfort zone and pray life-changing prayers for the people around me. I will do whatever You ask. Amen.

In becoming disciples of Jesus, we make the conscious decision to take on His yoke and participate in His redemptive mission to bring heaven to Earth. In making this leap of faith, we knowingly choose to take on the yoke of Christ in exchange for the burdensome yoke of this world. The freedom we find by taking on Jesus' yoke is greater than we could ever imagine!

CHAPTER 5

A TOWEL

A talmid is an intercessor in the truest sense of the word. They seek the success of others. They stand between heaven and Earth to discover the heart of God in particular situations and to pray His will into reality.

—Uncommon Favor

PATHWAY

Selflessness is a rare commodity. From the world's point of view, choosing others' needs over our own is unusual. But as we walk into our new life as fully surrendered talmidim, we find that Jesus' yoke is all about placing others above self. Our goal in this chapter is to actively become like Jesus in serving and seeking the success of others.

LANDMARKS

- Talmidim face complex problems and ask God to provide what they need to help others. As we exchange personal ambition for the heart of Jesus, God gives us a deep love for the people we are called to serve, and we seek their success above personal gain.
- A talmid is quick to forgive and enters into the journey of those around them, loving people in spite of—and even through—their imperfections.
- God brings unlikely relationships together to pioneer and establish specific platforms for impacting communities, cities, and nations.

KEY

It was just before the Passover Festival. Jesus knew that the hour had come for him to leave this world and go to the Father. Having loved his own who were in the world, he loved them to the end. The evening meal was in progress, and the devil had already prompted Judas, the son of Simon Iscariot, to betray Jesus. Jesus knew that the Father had put all things under his power, and that he had come from God and was returning to God; so he got up from the meal, took off his outer clothing, and wrapped a towel around his waist. After that, he poured water into a basin and began to wash his disciples' feet, drying them with the towel that was wrapped around him. He came to Simon Peter, who said to him, "Lord, are you going to wash my feet?" Jesus replied, "You do not realize now what I am doing, but later you will understand." "No," said Peter, "you shall never wash my feet." Jesus answered, "Unless I wash you, you have no part with me." "Then, Lord," Simon Peter replied, "not just my feet but my hands and my head as well!" Jesus answered, "Those who have had a bath need only to wash their feet; their whole body is clean. And you are clean, though not every one of you." For he knew who was going to betray him, and that was why he said not everyone was clean. When he had finished washing their feet, he put on his clothes and returned to his place. "Do you understand what I have done for you?" he asked them. "You call me 'Teacher' and 'Lord,' and rightly so, for that is what I am. Now that I, your Lord and Teacher, have washed your feet, you also should wash one another's feet. I have set you an example that you should do as I have done for you. Very truly I tell you, no servant is greater than his master, nor is a messenger greater than the one who sent him. Now that you know these things, you will be blessed if you do them." —John 13:1–17

This event occurred during the last days of Jesus' life on Earth. He had spent several years teaching, performing miracles, and imparting His yoke. It is here at the end that He emphasized the most important lessons to His disciples.

After He went around the room and washed their feet, He encouraged His talmidim to wash one another's feet. He added, "I have set you an example that you should do as I have done for you" (vv. 14–15). Then He followed up that command with a promise: "Now that you know these things, you will be blessed if you do them" (v. 17).

JOURNEY

KEEP YOUR TOWEL HANDY

Essentially, Jesus told His disciples that to become like Him and take on His yoke, His talmidim had to seek the success of others. He wants us to get inside the skin of those on the journey with us, for us to know one another deeply—weaknesses, sins, and all—and to make love our focus, keeping our towel of forgiveness handy.

1. When you think about serving others in your life, who comes to mind? Do you struggle to put their needs before your own? Why might this be difficult? What practical, small steps can you take to begin seeking the success of these people?

FORGIVENESS

It can be easier for us to envision serving the ones we love or those who are good to us. For example, you might be thinking, *I am going to start putting my wife's needs before my own and seek her success first because I love her and I want to honor her.* This is right and *necessary*. After all, Jesus was on the ground washing His friends' feet. But what about the person who isn't easy to love? Let's take that a step further—what about your enemy? Jesus spent three years in close friendship with Judas, the one who would betray Him. Jesus knew Judas would do this the entire time, and yet Jesus served Judas and loved him in the same way He loved and served the other disciples.

Forgiving people is difficult at times, especially when they have no idea how they have affected you. Forgiveness takes courage, initiative, and the choice to not withhold love. It is the only way to protect and preserve relationships and fulfill destiny together. We can better serve others when we have forgiven them.

2. Think over the events of your life. Are you harboring offense and unforgiveness toward anyone? Do you need to lay down anger, bitterness, and/or pride? What steps can you take to begin forgiving these people?

COUNTERCULTURE

> A dispute also arose among them as to which of them was considered to be greatest. Jesus said to them, "The kings of the Gentiles lord it over them; and those who exercise authority over them call themselves Benefactors. But you are not to be like that. Instead, the greatest among you should be like the youngest, and the one who rules like the one who serves. For who is greater, the one who is at the table or the one who serves? Is it not the one who is at the table? But I am among you as one who serves."—Luke 22:24–27

These verses reveal another conversation that occurred the night of the foot washing at the Passover dinner. The disciples were arguing over who was the greatest among them. Can you imagine living with Jesus for three years and still being concerned about position and prestige? But His talmidim were human, just like we are. In today's culture of image and power, it is easy for us too to grow self-absorbed and focus on our dreams and goals. Jesus was clear in these verses though: we are not meant to be like the rest of the world in this regard. There is no room among Jesus' disciples for competition, self-aggrandizement, or unforgiveness. The greatest one is the one who serves.

3. In what ways do you see culture perpetuating self-aggrandizement? How do these verses challenge the way you are currently living your life? What would it look like for you to lay down your ambitions to serve others first?

UNLIKELY ALLIANCES

When we take the posture of a servant and truly seek the success of others, God has room to forge unlikely but powerful alliances. Take Jesus' original twelve disciples, for example. He collected a motley crew that ranged from tax collectors to fishermen. They did not seem to have much in common, but Jesus trained them up and used them for the purpose of spreading the gospel to build His church. Change often happens when disparate people come together, and God is an expert at weaving people together to create change.

4. Who has God called you to partner with in an unlikely alliance? What vision has He given you for your greater purpose? How do you think God is trying to work through this alliance?

DESTINATION

Jesus, I pray for a humble heart that is willing to serve. Show me the people in my life whose needs I must put before my own. Make this my reality and help me forsake all selfish ambition. I release every desire to be recognized and successful according to others. And, Lord, show me those I need to forgive so I can better serve them. Thank You for calling us into partnership with other people. You alone, Lord, forge unlikely alliances and weave our stories together so we can make a difference for Your kingdom. As Your talmid, I am dedicated to being an intercessor and seeking the success of others. Amen.

In this chapter, the towel represents our servanthood as we seek the success of others, forgive them, and place their needs before our own. In this place of humility, God can begin to use us to influence His kingdom to a greater degree.

CHAPTER 6

LECH LECHAH: GO YOU

Sometimes we have to start with a blank page and no sense of direction, like Abraham when God said to him, "Lech Lechah!"—or "Go, you!" Yet God provided Abraham no direction until he actually packed up his belongings and began to move.

—Uncommon Favor

PATHWAY

Ecclesiastes tells us there is a time and a season for everything, including life and death, activity and rest. However, when God's talmidim answer His call to deeper discipleship, decisive action is required. Therefore, we must be prepared to get up and go when God says, "Go!"—even when we do not know where, why, or how.

LANDMARKS

- A disciple follows Jesus—not a vocation, a vision, or even a calling. Talmidim are always ready for Jesus' assignments. God leads His talmidim into impossible assignments to break ground, open up heaven's possibilities, and bring change where it is needed.

- Talmidim go when Jesus sends them, even when they don't fully understand where they are going, because they trust their rabbi. We do not have to know exactly what we are doing, but we do have to show up and move forward based on what little we do know.

- Jesus led His disciples into a relationship with Him that would impact their world, even though their efforts may have felt insignificant to them at the time. God is attracted to courage and faith, no matter how small.

KEY

The Lord had said to Abram, "Go from your country, your people and your father's household to the land I will show you. "I will make you into a great nation, and I will bless you; I will make your name great, and you will be a blessing. I will bless those who bless you, and whoever curses you I will curse; and all peoples on earth will be blessed through you." So Abram went, as the Lord had told him; and Lot went with him. Abram was seventy-five years old when he set out from Harran. He took his wife Sarai, his nephew Lot, all the possessions they had accumulated and the people they had acquired in Harran, and they set out for the land of Canaan, and they arrived there. Abram traveled through the land as far as the site of the great tree of Moreh at Shechem. At that time the Canaanites were in the land. The Lord appeared to Abram and said, "To your offspring I will give this land." So he built an altar there to the Lord, who had appeared to him. From there he went on toward the hills east of Bethel and pitched his tent, with Bethel on the west and Ai on the east. There he built an altar to the Lord and called on the name of the Lord. Then Abram set out and continued toward the Negev.
—Genesis 12:1-9

God made it clear from the beginning that to follow Him, His disciples would have to commit to a unique lifestyle. Part of that commitment is making selfless decisions that are incomprehensible to those seeking self-fulfillment. God requires a sacrificial life. Only in that place of sacrifice can He expand our resources and equip us to do the things Jesus Himself did. This sacrifice takes many different forms. Sometimes the sacrifice is leaving everything you know in pursuit of God's call.

JOURNEY

GOD INITIATES THE ASSIGNMENT

In Genesis 12 we see yet another rhythm for how God calls His talmidim into action. In verse 1, God told Abram (later Abraham) to leave everything behind and go to a new land that God would show him. The journey always begins with God initiating an assignment, and when God gives you one, He typically only reveals the first step. This is the mysterious way He chooses to work. Imagine hearing such a command from God. God then continued, "I will make you into a great nation" (v. 2). Remember, God always backs up His commands with a promise. However, He does not give us the whole picture. Abraham could never have known that the "great nation" God described would be His chosen people, the Jews, through whom He would send His Son, the Messiah, to redeem the whole earth.

1. God leads His talmidim into impossible assignments to break ground, open heaven's possibilities, and accomplish God's agenda in this world. Has God spoken to you or placed a burden on your heart for such an assignment? What have you heard Him say? What promises has He given you?

UNCOMMON FAVOR

God followed up with a promise to Abraham that he would live under a supernatural blessing. God essentially said, "If you do what I ask, then you will live a life of uncommon favor, and I will cause you to succeed." As you set out on the journey God has called you to, don't be surprised if you too live in the reality of uncommon favor. When God calls you to something, He will supply your every need and more.

2. How have you experienced God's supernatural blessing in your life? In what areas would you like to see more of God's favor? How would your life look different if you trusted that God would cause you to succeed with the assignment He has given to you?

FAITH TO BELIEVE

We continue to see the most essential element in this story—faith to believe what God says (see v. 7). Faith is woven throughout this journey from the beginning to the end, but we see it especially exemplified here. God told Abraham this was the land He would give to Abraham's offspring. But there were two problems: other people already inhabited the land, and Abraham and Sarah were far beyond childbearing years. However, rather than consider what seemed like impossibilities, Abraham built an altar to commemorate what God said. He had the faith to believe God would accomplish what He said He would do.

God is attracted to faith, no matter how small. He will honor our small ounce of faith and multiply it into something much greater.

3. What might be keeping you from completely believing what God is saying to you? What would it look like for you to step into a deeper level of faith for what He is asking you to do?

DAILY DEPENDENCE

There is a key element in Abraham's journey of faith that cannot be overlooked. We saw him step out in faith to begin the journey, but it is in verses 8 and 9 that we see how Abraham lived out the process. He took one step, stopped, and then called on the name of the Lord. This is critical. As disciples, we take baby steps and do the job right in front of us. But we have to hear from God along the way to keep moving. His greatest delight is in our daily dependence. It keeps us close to Him, in His intimate presence.

4. What is your process like as you respond to God's calling on your life? How are you seeking God's voice for His wisdom and next steps?

DESTINATION

God, I pray that You will reveal Your assignment to me. Show me where You are telling me to go! Give me ears to hear Your voice and use me as Your disciple to advance Your kingdom. I lay down all my selfish desires and ask You to help move me into a sacrificial response. Thank You, Lord, that You would choose to partner with me to accomplish Your will. I pray that You boldly send me into the unique and unknown assignment of my life. Jesus, I ask You to give me eyes to see the favor You have put on my life. Help me to believe You want me to succeed. God, I pray that You would remove every obstacle in my life that keeps me from stepping out in faith. I know all You ask is for a small amount of belief that You will do what You say. Grow this inside of me and help me when my doubt creeps in. I know You are a faithful God, and You bring all Your promises to completion. Amen.

Abraham's life and legacy are unrivaled except by that of Jesus Himself. But Abraham was called to simply listen and follow. These are the same tasks Jesus' talmidim are given. We listen, we hear God's command, we step out in action to follow, and we stop to listen again. While this sounds elementary, it is the rhythm for living a life of supernatural and uncommon favor.

CHAPTER 7

TOGETHER

Jesus knew His talmidim would need one another, not just for companionship, but as a band of brothers and sisters called into battle together.

—Uncommon Favor

PATHWAY

A critical step in becoming a talmid of Jesus is understanding the powerful concept of favor. The goal of this chapter is to better understand what the favor of God looks like and the power of locking arms with other believers to see God's plans established in the earth.

LANDMARKS

- God entrusts His most important work to talmidim who work closely together in small groups around a common vision.

- A talmid's disciplined patterns of worship, prayer, faith, and friendship enable them to walk with one another with agility and grace.

- God illuminates complex problems and daunting challenges to His talmidim, and they lock arms, pray, and work together to see God's will established in a transformational way.

KEY

[God] took [Abraham] outside and said, "Look up at the sky and count the stars—if indeed you can count them." Then he said to him, "So shall your offspring be." Abram believed the Lord, and He credited it to him as righteousness. He also said to him, "I am the Lord, who brought you out of Ur of the Chaldeans to give you this land to take possession of it." But Abram said, "Sovereign Lord, how can I know that I will gain possession of it?" So the Lord said to him, "Bring me a heifer, a goat and a ram, each three years old, along with a dove and a young pigeon." Abram brought all these to him, cut them in two and arranged the halves opposite each other; the birds, however, he did not cut in half. Then birds of prey came down on the carcasses, but Abram drove them away. As the sun was setting, Abram fell into a deep sleep, and a thick and dreadful darkness came over him. Then the Lord said to him, "Know for certain that for four hundred years your descendants will be strangers in a country not their own and that they will be enslaved and mistreated there. But I will punish the nation they serve as slaves, and afterward they will come out with great possessions." —Genesis 15:5-14

JOURNEY

When Abraham followed God's call to go to the land of Canaan, he took with him a community of people who supported his mission and lived under the immediate blessings of God, just as Abraham did. Abraham did not become the father of a great nation and the spiritual mediator of blessings to the world by himself. His group of three-hundred-plus friends, family members, and servants were his community of believers who took an active role in the mission and contributed to the transformation taking place at the time. God favored Abraham and the group of people who were with him. He chose Abraham to embody for future generations what blessing and favor look like from God's perspective.

When you study Genesis chapters 12–24, you'll discover that there were different levels of favor and blessing on Abraham's life, three in particular. First, God gave him personal blessings of protection, provision, and friendship. Then He blessed those who interacted with him and his mission. Abraham also received blessings for the whole human race through his obedience.

So, what brought God's favor and blessing into Abraham's life? Consider the following.

HIS CALL

Little did Abraham know that his decision to listen to and obey the Lord would affect entire nations and kingdoms to come. Written around two millennia later, Hebrews 11:8-12 tells us:

> By faith Abraham, when called to go to a place he would later receive as his inheritance, obeyed and went, even though he did not know where he was going. By faith he made his home in the promised land like a stranger in a foreign country; he lived in tents, as did Isaac and Jacob, who were heirs with him of the same promise. For he was looking forward to the city with foundations, whose architect and builder is God. And by faith even Sarah, who was past childbearing age, was enabled to bear children because she considered Him faithful who had made the promise. And so from this one man, and he as good as dead, came descendants as numerous as the stars in the sky and as countless as the sand on the seashore.

Abraham was called to surrender his social circle and to leave his land, family, and traditions. He was moved by divine guidance into a new land to receive the promise and blessing of becoming the father of a new nation. In foregoing certain earthly securities, Abraham was ushered into blessings of a far greater magnitude.

1. What earthly securities have you given up to align yourself with God's promises and destiny over your life and that of your family?

HIS LIFESTYLE

Read all of Genesis 15 for a clearer understanding of what God gave Abraham.

God formed a covenant with Abraham that centered on two things: making him into a great nation with many descendants and giving him a specific land to occupy. Even though Abraham did not own the land during his lifetime, he obeyed God by walking the territory as an act of prayer over the future, and he built altars to the Lord.

2. In the previous chapter you answered a question about the active steps of faith you are taking because of what you believe God has shown you to do. Are others involved in the process with you or are you taking those steps alone for now? What does it feel like? Explain.

HIS COMMUNITY

By faith, Abraham became an intercessor for a huge, unseen, future community (Jews and Gentiles). Yet in his lifetime, he was head of a covenant community that lived under the immediate blessing of God (Eliezer, Lot, Sarah, Isaac, Hagar, Ishmael, etc.).

3. Are you connected to a group of people who are committed to working and praying together to influence or transform society? If so, what do you believe is the group's mission, and why are you drawn to be a part of it? What are your practical next steps of contributing your time, talent, and treasure to the mission?

PRAYER

Father God, You did not create me to go through this life as Your talmid alone. Your Word says that when two or more are gathered, You are there also. Lead me to divine connections, reveal those safe relationships in my life, and weave together a group of talmidim with whom I can bond, grow, and pursue Your kingdom purposes. I know You have built Your kingdom on the foundation of fellow Christ-followers working together in unity, as one, to accomplish Your purposes in the earth. Show me who You have brought along for me to take the journey with—allow me to clearly see who my group is and how we can move into the specific assignment You have for us. Amen.

DESTINATION

The significant thing to remember about Abraham is that God's blessing was linked to his faith lifestyle. He took seriously the call to obey God and walk intimately with Him, and he was joined together with a faith community that had set themselves toward a specific mission and purpose.

1. If you are not connected to a small group of talmidim as mentioned above, do you believe you are supposed to start your own?

2. If so, what would the mission be, who would you like to be a part of it with you, and what would you like to see happen?

3. The journey begins with one step. What is the next step you need to take to build or join a committed community of talmidim?

CHAPTER 8

FINDING HOME

We can construct an impressive identity—a vision of grandeur about ourselves—and the world around us can buy into it, only to realize that on the inside we are as fragile as a house of cards. Relief comes from unvarnished honesty about ourselves as we hand our disappointments over to Jesus. Where we are most honest with God and ourselves, we find Him most intimately to be our Father and Healer.

—Uncommon Favor

PATHWAY

God has given us a kingdom of fellow talmidim in which we can find hope and companionship. His will is for us to invest ourselves in significant spiritual relationships that help us heal from the past, mature spiritually, and equip us to go forth courageously.

LANDMARKS

- God gives us significant relationships to help shape our identity, and these relationships are our primary platform for personal development.
- Our personal healing and transformation cannot happen amid resistance, anger, or pride—only in transparent humility.
- Our failures enable us to see the truth about ourselves and ultimately strengthen our identity as we give ourselves more fully to Him.

KEY

> When they had finished eating, Jesus said to Simon Peter, "Simon son of John, do you love me more than these?" "Yes, Lord," he said, "you know that I love you." Jesus said, "Feed my lambs." Again Jesus said, "Simon son of John, do you love me?" He answered, "Yes, Lord, you know that I love you." Jesus said, "Take care of my sheep." The third time he said to him, "Simon son of John, do you love me?" Peter was hurt because Jesus asked him the third time, "Do you love me?" He said, "Lord, you know all things; you know that I love you." Jesus said, "Feed my sheep." —John 21:15–17

This was after the resurrection—after Peter denied his rabbi three times. Can you imagine the shame and rejection Peter must have felt after denying his Master and now seeing Him again face to face? But Jesus was there, sitting with him on the shore, having a meal around a fire. In this intimate setting Jesus asked Peter—three times—if he loved Him. Jesus created a safe place where Peter could be fully reconciled to Him again. This exchange profoundly affected Peter's life. Indeed, one of the primary ways God redeems our lives is through meaningful, safe friendships where our wounds can heal and we can become our unique selves, fully free of our past.

1. Who has shaped you most positively and plays that role right now in your life?

2. What is your image or impression of God when you pray to Him? Do you feel close to Him, or do you feel distant from Him? Do you feel judged by Him or received by Him? What goes on inwardly and emotionally when you have a setback in life?

3. Peter understood something significant about Jesus that enabled him to forego self-hatred and make his courageous swim to shore. What do you think that was? What failure might be holding you back from believing you are fully accepted and forgiven? What would need to happen for you to change your thinking and close the gap you feel between you and God?

4. In John 21:15 what do you think Jesus was affirming in Peter when He asked him, "Simon son of John, do you love me more than these?"

Reread verses 15–23 and walk through the process as if you were standing in Peter's shoes.

5. What would you be thinking? What was Jesus doing with Peter, and what was Jesus' main point? What invitation was Peter accepting?

PRAYER

Father, I want to be received as I am and not as I should be. I want a change in my perception of You. I know I can do nothing to reverse my failures and their impact on me and others, but I want to swim to shore, fully believing You know how to do the deep, mysterious work to heal me and those around me. I want to be overshadowed by the fire of Your love and transformed deep inside. I accept that I will never have my act together, but, in trust, I turn to Jesus' shed blood that has made me completely righteous and forgiven. I fully release my concerns, habits, dreams, and relationships to You. I want to live with the same confidence as Peter, knowing I am irreversibly and compassionately loved by You. Amen.

DESTINATION

Peter played a central role in the gospel's going forth into the world, but first Jesus spent time with him reviewing the foundations of life—who Jesus is and His message—in such a way that Peter would never be the same.

1. Do you ever feel like Peter—as if you have let God down or somehow disappointed Him? How and when?

2. Jesus lavished forgiveness upon Peter in a very real and intimate way. In what ways do you need to allow Jesus into your most wounded or damaged areas?

3. What message does God want you to receive from Him about your identity and who you are in relation to others?

CHAPTER 9

SOLITUDE, SILENCE, AND LISTENING

We are not superstars. We need rest and solitude—each year, each week, and some part of each day. If we were convinced that the true essence of our being and our far-reaching accomplishments were contingent on our time of solitude with God, wouldn't we make it our chief priority?

—Uncommon Favor

PATHWAY

In your desire to grow as a talmid and become the person God designed you to be, you learn to embrace the disciplines of solitude, silence, and listening so your soul can be renewed and you can hear clearly from God.

LANDMARKS

- The discipline of regular solitude (daily, weekly, monthly, yearly, etc.) is our most restorative practice, and a talmid creates an environment conducive to listening. Obedience requires a listening heart.

- Pushing ourselves beyond our limits leads to exhaustion, and prolonged exhaustion impacts our will, our choices, and our personality. It degrades our character and slowly bankrupts our human desires.

- Our human limitations actually allow us to focus and grow deeper roots, and a talmid understands the unique ways God speaks to them.

KEY

My sheep listen to my voice; I know them, and they follow me. I give them eternal life, and they shall never perish; no one will snatch them out of my hand. My Father, who has given them to me, is greater than all; no one can snatch them out of my Father's hand. I and the Father are one. —John 10:27-30

JOURNEY

In solitude we come to know the Holy Spirit. With Him, we can simplify our lives on the inside and out and create space for change and growth. This is where our inner freedom grows. And we see that this was important to Jesus. He went to lonely places to pray, to find rest, and to restore His confidence in who He was and what He had been sent to do. In solitude we recover our true identity. We unmask false impressions about ourselves and others, and we settle down to the still small voice that has been begging to be heard.

Many people are lonely in life, but God desires to take our aching loneliness and transform it into something beautiful and meaningful with Him.

Our approach to solitude involves cultivating an expectation for what He will reveal to us. His Word and His Spirit have a very powerful relationship. The Holy Spirit wants to reveal the *rhema* of God (Spirit-breathed word in real time) and to illuminate the *logos* (the written word of God). This truth is clearly exemplified in Jesus' interaction with the two disciples He met on the road to Emmaus and then broke bread with: "They (the disciples) asked each other, 'Were not our hearts burning within us while He talked with us on the road and opened the Scriptures to us?'" (Luke 24:32).

Listening to the Holy Spirit is an integral part of a disciple's journey and the most natural response for every believer. Jesus put it eloquently when He said, "My sheep listen to my voice; I know them, and they follow me" (John 10:27).

Write out the following scriptures and underline what your expectation might be from God in your time of solitude with Him.

- Psalm 25:9

- Psalm 32:8

- Psalm 73:24

- Proverbs 8:34

Listening requires humble submission and being led instead of taking the lead. The biggest hurdle can be our minds, because we tend to have an affinity for our own thoughts. God wants to use our minds for His thoughts. Yet, if we are always thinking, analyzing, and mentally engaged, we forfeit the ability to hear Him.

As simple as it sounds, having a regular time and an undistracted place for meeting with God is necessary for cultivating a spiritual life where we can listen. When we have a plan, we put ourselves in an intentional posture for change and growth. Use the following as a practical exercise in learning to listen to the Holy Spirit's counsel through God's Word.

This exercise below can be applied to any passage of Scripture that you are reading. It is meant to lead you into being able to listen closely to what the Holy Spirit is saying to you.

APPROACHING SOLITUDE

1. Quiet your heart. This first involves releasing our fears. Fear is a distraction and takes on the form of excessive thinking about people, circumstances, and the future. Quieting ourselves involves receiving God's love into the places of our hearts and minds where we are inclined to fear. What fears do you need to release to Him? List them and turn them over to Him.

> Take time to boldly declare His love over your circumstances—those that have yet to happen as well as those that have already occurred. Add some calm, worshipful music to slow your mental paces and quiet your heart before God. Ask God to give you peace (see Psalm 46:10; Isaiah 30:15).

One of the most faith-building passages in all of Scripture is 1 John 5:14–15: "This is the confidence we have in approaching God that if we ask anything according to His will, He hears us. And if we know that He hears us—whatever we ask—we know we have what we have asked of Him." Since we know it is God's will for us to hear Him, we can pray this verse in expectation that He will speak to us.

2. Ask Him to counsel you. Contemplate the psalmist's words in Psalm 32:8 and turn them into a prayer: "Thank You, Lord, that You will instruct me and teach me in the way I should go. You will counsel me with Your eye upon me."

3. Rely on Him to lead you into His Word. Ask Him to draw your attention to a particular book of the Bible and then plan to stay in that book for several days or weeks. What book do you feel like He is leading you to? Go to that book and begin at chapter one.Read gently. Being counseled in His Word will involve reading little portions each day and listening to what He is saying about it as it relates to you, a circumstance in your life, or someone you know. The Holy Spirit will likely give you wisdom and then guide you to help someone else. Read gently while waiting patiently for God to speak to your heart. In this way, we practice stillness and listening with our spirit. Read a paragraph or two and stop when you feel like the Holy Spirit is leading you to do so. The aim in this exercise is not to study or read for comprehension; you are asking the Holy Spirit to do what He does best, which is to counsel you through His Word as it relates to your personal life. (See Isaiah 50:4.)

4. Jot down the verse or verses that stand out the most. Read them again and again. What do you sense He is saying to you about those verses?

5. Now, ask yourself: What is the significant truth being spoken about in this passage? How does this apply to my life right now? What, if anything, do I need to do about this today or this week? Write down what He shows you and pray over it. The next day you will pick up from where you left off with another portion of the Scripture.

6. Set a short-term goal to apply what He has shown you. Ask the Holy Spirit for grace to follow through in a practical way. Take time to surrender to Him and to His will. Our solitude becomes an overflow into our community, family, and circumstances. The Holy Spirit may lead you to write a letter, make a phone call, throw a party, or develop a prayer life around the promises He is giving to you personally or for others. Jesus' ministry was the outcome of His solitude and oneness with God. Yours will be too. The Holy Spirit will empower you to influence others through your time with Him.

DESTINATION

Father God, help me to take the time to slow down, quiet my heart, and sit in Your presence. I cannot hear You clearly through the constant static of everyday life, and I know my intimacy with You depends on my ability to sit quietly in Your presence. Father, help me surrender any shame or guilt I have about the past for times when I did not seek Your presence. I want to embrace You now—I yearn to connect with You, Father, and to feel and embrace Your love. Outside of You is darkness, Lord. Help me seek Your light each day through a quiet place, a quiet time, and a quiet heart. For I know that as I seek places and times of silence and tune my spirit to hear You, You will embrace, guide, and instruct me. Amen.

Embracing the Holy Spirit and the Word together becomes a dynamic combination for receiving the Lord's counsel and instruction about our present circumstances. Cultivating a listening ear is a tangible act of true surrender to His will above our own. The more we enter into solitude and quiet our mind, the more we will hear from God. He yearns to speak to us—to develop us, mature us, and empower us to bear much fruit.

CHAPTER 10

TRUE AUTHORITY

He expanded the horizon of love for humanity and showed His talmidim that the kingdom of God stands above and beyond ethical rules, and He explained that it would likely disrupt their everyday world in completely unpredictable ways.

—Uncommon Favor

PATHWAY

When we grow closer to the Father as His talmidim, His priorities become our priorities. His concerns become our concerns. In this growth process, we come to understand that love and compassion are the most effective and influential positions of all, far above earthly titles and designated roles of authority.

LANDMARKS

- People need to be validated and loved where they are and for who they are. Love extracts the treasure in people whether they deserve it or not.

- Compassion and true love become the core—even the very nature—of authority. This love will go beyond cultural norms and preconceived notions. Jesus' talmidim embrace a radical commitment to love that changes society.

- We learn to answer the call to represent Jesus on Earth in our spheres of influence, and it is our job to find out how and where God wants us involved.

KEY

On one occasion an expert in the law stood up to test Jesus. "Teacher," he asked, "what must I do to inherit eternal life?" "What is written in the Law?" he replied. "How do you read it?" He answered, "'Love the Lord your God with all your heart and with all your soul and with all your strength and with all your mind'; and, 'Love your neighbor as yourself.'" "You have answered correctly," Jesus replied. "Do this and you will live." But he wanted to justify himself, so he asked Jesus, "And who is my neighbor?" In reply Jesus said: "A man was going down from Jerusalem to Jericho, when he was attacked by robbers. They stripped him of his clothes, beat him and went away, leaving him half dead. A priest happened to be going down the same road, and when he saw the man, he passed by on the other side. So too, a Levite, when he came to the place and saw him, passed by on the other side. But a Samaritan, as he traveled, came where the man was; and when he saw him, he took pity on him. He went to him and bandaged his wounds, pouring on oil and wine. Then he put the man on his own donkey, brought him to an inn and took care of him. The next day he took out two denarii and gave them to the innkeeper. 'Look after him,' he said, 'and when I return, I will reimburse you for any extra expense you may have.' "Which of these three do you think was a neighbor to the man who fell into the hands of robbers?" The expert in the law replied, "The one who had mercy on him." Jesus told him, "Go and do likewise." —Luke 10:25-37

JOURNEY

We cannot hope to make an impact on the world without compassion. Compassion is deep sympathy for someone or a group of people, accompanied by a strong need to relieve them from a harmful circumstance. Compassion goes beyond feelings to action.

Jesus' life was marked by compassion. He frequently violated the rules and proper conduct of His own society, not just through His connections with the Samaritans but also with tax collectors, women of questionable reputation, the insane, the dead, and so on. He expanded the horizon of love for humanity and showed His talmidim that the kingdom of God stands above ethical rules and would likely disrupt their everyday world in unpredictable ways.

WHO IS YOUR NEIGHBOR?

1. Has there been a distinct time in your life when someone has shown you compassion when you really needed it? How did it change your view of your circumstances? How did it affect your view of God?

2. Go a step further. Who has been a Good Samaritan to you? Who has set aside time to help you heal or be delivered from a painful circumstance, addiction, or relationship? What personal sacrifices did they make for you? How did that change your life?

3. To whom have you been a Good Samaritan, where you made sacrifices for someone who is not a family member or close friend, one who is outside your social circle? How did it impact them emotionally and spiritually? What were they able to do because of your compassion toward them?

The Good Samaritan is an unlikely hero. He traveled into "fringe" territory between two cultures—not to fulfill a duty but to answer a call by God. The Samaritan was moved by compassion for the man in the ditch. He stepped beyond the rules and rhetoric of his day to save another person's life. In the culture of the day, the Jew and the Samaritan should have despised each other, but instead the Good Samaritan sought out a personal relationship with the wounded Jew.

4. Who are your unlikely "neighbors"? Who might God be calling you to reach out to outside of your immediate social circle and sphere of influence? How might you develop a friendship with them or get involved with them in some way? How do you think you could be a source of healing to them or an asset to their family?

UNCOMMON FAVOR STUDY JOURNAL

PRAYER

Jesus, Your life was filled and marked with compassion. Without Your love and compassion for me, I would be nowhere. Please overshadow my life and my desires with compassion for those You want me to be personally involved with. Soften my heart to see my neighbor and show me how to be a source of healing and strength to them. Open my eyes to see how to care for them practically. Amen.

5. **Read John 13:34–35.** What new command did Jesus give His disciples? This verse reveals the centerpiece of His interpretation of the whole Law of Moses.

6. **Read 1 John 4:7-21.** How did John link our love for others while on Earth to our confidence about the final judgment day? What did he say?

7. "God is love." From this place of understanding, how can you make God's love credible to those around you in practical ways? Is there anyone from whom you are intentionally withholding love?

DESTINATION

Jesus, I long to live my life compelled by love. I invite You to transform my thoughts, actions, and motivations when it comes to my heart for others. Help me live a life marked by compassion and radical love. Help me to deeply forgive the offenses inside of my heart toward _____ . Open my eyes to those around me and show me where I can make Your love credible in my own world. I want my authority in this life to come from my compassion so that the world might know You. Amen.

As a talmid who has joined in Jesus' mission on Earth, we understand that there is no way to authentically love those around us without entering into their messy lives. The love Jesus gave the outcast and sinner went beyond a tithe, donation, or a few kind words. He took action to restore them, heal them, and have meals with them.

We look for ways to do the same and to break out of our comfort zones. His love and compassion—given through His Holy Spirit—allow us to take actions we would otherwise be unwilling or unable to take.

CHAPTER 11

OVERCOMING EVIL

From the beginning of their journey with God, talmidim of Jesus need to understand the strategic ways Satan and his emissaries operate, and they need to be able to overcome demonic influences.

—Uncommon Favor

PATHWAY

"Greater is He who is in us than he who is in the world" (1 John 4:4, author's paraphrase). While keeping this in mind, it is critical that we know our adversary. We must learn to walk confidently in our victorious position as disciples of Jesus.

LANDMARKS

- We must remember that we are destined for victory. As disciples of Jesus, we approach warfare from the position of victory. We are promised that we are made more than conquerors through Christ Jesus (see Romans 8:37).

- The Bible confirms that demons—fallen angels who work against the purposes of God—are indeed real. Evil spirits attempt to influence people to rely on their intellect and reason by idolizing religious concepts that are void of a personal experience with God. Demonic spirits seek to penetrate our emotions and attitudes to deceive us. However, they are only as powerful as the extent to which we agree with them by exchanging the voice of truth for the voices of deception. We must know what God's voice sounds like.

- While we are all vulnerable to spiritual attack, God's Word assures us that He will protect us from the enemy, and that we will come out on the other side of battle strengthened and victorious.

- A talmid of Jesus needs to consider the battles they will enter if they choose to be His disciple. Once they make that choice, they need a reliable plan—a daily practice and rhythm that prepare them to face the adversary by immersing them in the truth found in God's Word.

KEY

Be alert and of sober mind. Your enemy the devil prowls around like a roaring lion looking for someone to devour. Resist him, standing firm in the faith, because you know that the family of believers throughout the world is undergoing the same kind of sufferings. And the God of all grace, who called you to his eternal glory in Christ, after you have suffered a little while, will himself restore you and make you strong, firm and steadfast. —1 Peter 5:8–10

JOURNEY

It is critical that we understand our position in heaven if we want to understand how to overcome evil. Scripture tells us that we are made more than conquerors through Christ Jesus. On the cross, the cries of Jesus announced the triumph—it was finished. As co-heirs with Christ, we are partakers in His victory (see Romans 8:17).

As we encounter demonic forces that seek to usurp the truth of that victory by sowing seeds of fear, doubt, anger, offense, and frustration, we must remind ourselves of where we are seated.

We see in the verses above that even though the enemy prowls around like a lion, the Lord has provided a way to overcome his schemes. God is the ultimate Lion, the Lion of the Tribe of Judah, and He is roaring over us with a banner of victory. We are called to be alert, submitting ourselves to God and resisting the devil. When we do this, the enemy has no choice but to flee. Jesus Himself modeled this when Satan tempted Him in the desert. Matthew 4:1–11 describes Jesus as being tempted three times by Satan. If you read this passage, you will notice what Jesus did each time to combat the enemy's lies: He quoted God's Word.

Remember: You are already equipped with the most powerful tools in your spiritual arsenal— Scripture and prayer.

These emissaries or spirits of the satanic realm cannot indwell a true believer in Jesus Christ. But they can influence and deceive. Satan and his fallen angels can certainly oppress Christians. We can see this clearly when Peter, James, and John were deceived in the garden of Gethsemane and deserted Jesus out of fear for their lives.

1. In what ways have you seen the enemy "prowling around" in your life? What feelings of fear, doubt, anger, and offense have you experienced? Have you felt like you have been under an oppressive spirit? If so, what did that feel like?

2. What practical steps can you take to become more alert to the schemes of the enemy? How would your life look different if you took an offensive position against the enemy? How would you face a battle if you knew that ultimately it was already won?

READ LUKE 22:54–57.

In this passage, we see Peter—who later became filled with great boldness to empower the church—cower in fear and deny Jesus. We also see this in the Old Testament after Elijah boldly defeated the priests of Baal, only to run away in fear from a wicked woman who threatened to have him killed (see 1 Kings 17–19). Amid our failures and the enemy's schemes to thwart God's work in our lives, God is still wiser. He is forever ruining the strategies of the enemy and fulfilling His eternal purposes. Where the enemy thought he had won in causing the most vocal of Jesus' disciples to deny Him, Jesus used that moment to bring true redemption to Peter and inspire future generations who would fall prey to the same temptations. Indeed, God does work all things together for the good of those who love Him (see Romans 8:28).

KNOW WHERE YOUR ENEMY IS

It is easy to think of evil forces in places we consider evil, but we don't often think of Satan waging war in our small groups, homes, or cooking clubs. We are vulnerable to evil spirits in our moments of weakness, when we are sad, lonely or even just tired. We can see that vulnerability reflected in the life of Judas, who walked closely with Christ. He was susceptible to the enemy's lies because he ran away from Christ instead of running to Christ when he was faced with temptation.

Through Judas, perhaps God wants us to remember that the presence of evil can be at work even in the circles of Jesus' dearest disciples. However, there is a choice to come into agreement with the lies of the enemy that would sow seeds of shame and separation.

Satan devises his most potent strategy for the areas where the gospel is advancing by making disciples feel isolated and alone. One of the greatest tools we have to combat the schemes of the enemy is to expose him by surrounding ourselves with healthy accountability and community.

3. Have you ever found yourself in a deep conflict and offense with a friend and wondered how you got there? The enemy loves to tear down every good relationship. How have you seen Satan at work in your family, friend groups, and social circles? What can you practically do to start waging war against the enemy in your sphere of influence?

4. Do you have someone you can trust to speak openly with about some of the lies you have been believing? Exposing lies and inviting truth takes away all the power of the enemy.

DISAPPOINTMENT WITH GOD

I think we would be hard-pressed to find a believer whose life turned out exactly as they thought it would. Life tends to be full of disappointment, and while this can definitely be emotionally difficult and trying, it is important for us to not get lost in the anger of our disappointment or allow seeds of bitterness to take root. There are times in life when we feel betrayed and upset by God. We can feel like we were doing what He asked us to do, following Him righteously, and yet the chair still gets pulled out from under us.

We are often left under a depressive cloud, wondering if God is good. The enemy loves to step into our disappointment by making us believe that God's intentions for us are not good. We must remember that He says He has plans to prosper us and not to harm us (see Jeremiah 29:11).

5. How have you felt disappointed with God? This is a vulnerable and sometimes painfully honest question to ask yourself. Bring it before Him. How can you begin to let go of that disappointment and move forward?

6. Would you be willing to walk through this disappointment with a friend and release any judgments you may have made toward God? For some, it might be helpful to write out your disappointments so you can read them to a safe confidant who can help you pray through and release them to God.

READ EPHESIANS 6:10–18.

> Finally, be strong in the Lord and in his mighty power. Put on the full armor of God, so that you can take your stand against the devil's schemes. For our struggle is not against flesh and blood, but against the rulers, against the authorities, against the powers of this dark world and against the spiritual forces of evil in the heavenly realms. Therefore put on the full armor of God, so that when the day of evil comes, you may be able to stand your ground, and after you have done everything, to stand. Stand firm then, with the belt of truth buckled around your waist, with the breastplate of righteousness in place, and with your feet fitted with the readiness that comes from the gospel of peace. In addition to all this, take up the shield of faith, with which you can extinguish all the flaming arrows of the evil one. Take the helmet of salvation and the sword of the Spirit, which is the word of God. And pray in the Spirit on all occasions with all kinds of prayers and requests. With this in mind, be alert and always keep on praying for all the Lord's people.

Notice that each piece of the armor of God in this passage is offensive—each piece is intended for a frontal confrontation with the enemy. This means, just like Jesus when He fought the devil head on with the Word of God, we need to stand firm and rely on the spiritual armor outlined in Ephesians 6 to protect us and bring us into victory over our enemy. Resistance is key. When we stand our ground as children of the almighty God, the devil will retreat. God's Word confirms this in James 4:7: "Submit yourselves, then, to God. Resist the devil, and he will flee from you."

DESTINATION

Father, thank You for working all things together for my good. Open my eyes to the work of Satan and his emissaries in my life and keep me alert and prepared for battle. Show me any places where I have allowed fear, offense, or any other emotion to keep me from experiencing the fullness of Your love. I submit my mind, will, and emotions to You, and I choose to trust You over any emotion or attitude. Reveal to me the schemes of the enemy and continue to draw me into Your love. I am sorry for the ways I have bought into the enemy's lies and allowed them to dictate areas of my life. I want to walk in Your truth! Amen.

One practical step that you can take is to "pray on" the armor of God every day. Wake up every morning, open your Bible to Ephesians 6, and pray through putting on each piece of the armor. This way, you can begin your day in a place of strength and alertness.

Remind yourself of where your seat is. Practice sitting in the seat of victory, with Satan under your feet. As you sit, ask God to remind you of who He says you are. You are more than a conqueror.

To be prepared for battle, talmidim need a daily plan and practice. The point of understanding the enemy's schemes isn't to fight the battle and conquer Satan alone. Instead, we learn to rely on God's strength, trusting Him based on what He said He will do. We pursue the Father and stay connected to the presence of God. There is no substitute for His presence in our pursuit to live victoriously.

CHAPTER 12

ADVANCING

The key to advancing God's kingdom is friendship with God.

—Uncommon Favor

PATHWAY

Do you think of yourself as a friend of God? For some, that concept may seem odd, but that is exactly what God desires with His talmidim. We need to understand that friendship with God through the Holy Spirit will become the main investment of our lives. The byproduct of our relationship with God is the advancement of His kingdom!

LANDMARKS

- To early talmidim, the Holy Spirit was vital, the inescapable imperative for every disciple and their ability to cooperate with God. And as they put the kingdom of God first, they discovered who they were in the process.
- To be on the King's highway every day is to care about what He cares about in the larger sense of the kingdom of heaven.
- In a dynamic friendship with us, the Holy Spirit leads us out to the edge of things to take risks for the sake of love.

KEY

I have much more to say to you, more than you can now bear. But when he, the Spirit of truth, comes, he will guide you into all the truth. He will not speak on his own; he will speak only what he hears, and he will tell you what is yet to come. He will glorify me because it is from me that he will receive what he will make known to you. All that belongs to the Father is mine. That is why I said the Spirit will receive from me what he will make known to you. —John 16:12–15

JOURNEY

Friendship with God is based on our level of intimacy with the Holy Spirit. As we open ourselves to know Him deeply and intimately, we plug into the bigger picture of what God is doing on Earth. As a result, we enlarge our identity and move away from a smaller version of ourselves. As we decrease so He may increase, the compelling question becomes, how do we participate in advancing the kingdom of God?

1. Read Luke 24:49. What did Jesus send His disciples to do? Why do you think He insisted on this step before they did anything else? How would this step be important to their advancing the kingdom?

2. Read John 16:7. Jesus commends the Advocate to His talmidim. Who is the Advocate, and how would He take the place of Jesus? How would the Advocate be better for the disciples than Jesus staying on the earth?

3. Reread John 16:12–15. What important role will the Holy Spirit play? What will He do? The word "mine" is used twice in these verses. It comes from the Greek word emos, which means "that which I possess." How will the Holy Spirit bring glory to Jesus and to His Father?

4. **Read John 16:13.** What specifically would the Holy Spirit tell the disciples?

It was not so easy to be a witness of Jesus in His day. But His disciples had been completely transformed. It was their highest privilege to lay down their lives for Him. They were not church growth strategists or eloquent speakers. They were simply aflame with love and under the influence of the Holy Spirit. Their reputations did not seem to matter to them. They had been given new identities that far exceeded what they could have produced or built for themselves.

The message of the kingdom of God spread like wildfire throughout the Roman Empire and beyond, and the flame inside these early witnesses simply could not be put out—not through persecution, sword, or by any other means.

One can only deduce from the book of Acts that the gospel impacted the world the way it did because the Holy Spirit worked so powerfully through the disciples. God's power had invaded their lives. In the span of just a few short years, the gospel had spread throughout most of the known world, from Jerusalem to Judea and to the uttermost parts of civilization. They had no New Testament to read, no devotional books, online courses, or promotional strategies.

The Holy Spirit who flowed unhindered through those early believers is the same Holy Spirit who transforms us today. His love, power, and guidance are the same yesterday, today, and tomorrow. He has been given the authority to embolden us and give us His power to impact culture and to bring transformational change into the world.

ADVANCING

Now go back a few steps. Jesus was sending His disciples to Jerusalem, where they would have a penetrating infusion of power from on high, to wait on the Holy Spirit.

READ LUKE 24:26–49 AND JOHN 20:19–22.

These two eyewitness accounts reveal a very unusual scene after Jesus' resurrection. He came through a wall in an upper room where His disciples were hiding.

5. What did He do that was so unusual? Why was this important? What do you think happened as a result?

6. **Reread Luke 24:45.** What else did Jesus do for His disciples? What do you think might have happened once He did this for them? How would this one miracle change everything for them?

7. **Reread Luke 24:49.** Why would the disciples need to stay in Jerusalem and wait on the Holy Spirit if they had just received the Holy Spirit when Jesus breathed on them? In some ways that doesn't make sense. What else did they need to receive from the Holy Spirit?

We can infer from the Scriptures that after they had received the Holy Spirit, there was still a dimension of the Holy Spirit that needed to be released to them. Jesus' command for them to wait in Jerusalem was for the purpose of baptizing them in the Holy Spirit. Only after Jesus ascended to heaven could He send the Holy Spirit to baptize them with power.

As the story goes, one hundred and twenty born-again Jewish talmidim gathered in Jerusalem with a new, very clear understanding of the Scriptures and with the Holy Spirit dwelling in them. They waited ten days while in prayer and expectation for the gift Jesus had promised them. Suddenly they heard a mighty rushing wind (see Acts 2). It filled the room, and what appeared as tongues of fire separated and rested on each of them. They began to speak in other tongues as the Spirit enabled them.

Jesus had prepared His talmidim for this special day when they would be "clothed with power from on high" so they could be His witnesses. To be like Him, they needed to be endowed with power by the Holy Spirit.

ADVANCING

8. **Read Joel 2:28–29 and Matthew 3:11.** What was prophesied about the Holy Spirit?

9. **Read 1 Corinthians 4:20.** What did Paul say about the importance of the Holy Spirit's power?

As you read the book of Acts, you will see that the early disciples had unprecedented encounters with the Holy Spirit. These Jewish talmidim valued every possible encounter with Him, and they stewarded the gifts they received from Him. They gave the Holy Spirit full control and priority in their lives. They maintained an atmosphere of expectancy, hunger, and thirst for all the Holy Spirit wanted to do in and through them. His power, gifts, and relationship with them would become an unfolding adventure for the rest of their lives.

10. How much of a role does the Holy Spirit play in your life? How much freedom and priority have you given Him? What identifiable supernatural gifts have you received from Him?

11. What would you be willing to do to have more of the Holy Spirit in your life, to receive His power and His gifts?

Jesus' talmidim arranged their lives around very personal encounters with the Holy Spirit. The Holy Spirit responds where He is longed for and wanted. Once the Holy Spirit initially comes into your life with power, you will know it. Then He comes again and again. The first encounter with Him is vital, and it opens the way for encounter after encounter with Him as a way of life.

THE KING'S HIGHWAY

Talmidim get out of balance quickly when they turn inward and center their prayers continuously around their own needs and lack. We get stuck when we do that. To be on the King's highway is to be connected to the movement of God where He is transforming societies all over the world. To be on His highway is to care about what He cares about in the larger sense of the kingdom of heaven.

12. What can you do to align yourself better with God's greater purposes? How can you incorporate the larger picture into your prayer life while keeping your personal needs before Him? How would being part of a bigger vision also enlarge your identity and who you are becoming?

DESTINATION

Holy Spirit, I humbly surrender everything to You—all of my desires and plans. I desperately want more of You. I want to be clothed in power and considered Your close friend. I don't want to be a lukewarm Christian. I give myself to You as a living sacrifice, like Your early talmidim did. I want the kind of relationship they had with You. I want to ask You to align my heart for an invasion of You into my personality, nature, and character. I want You to penetrate the depths of who I am, and I want to be led by You for the rest of my life. Amen.

God cooperates with His risk-taking friends. We take nervy steps of faith around what He reveals—whether in business, in politics, or at home—but God does the heavy lifting of bringing relationships together and changing hearts. In a dynamic friendship with the Holy Spirit, we are led out to the edge of things to take risks for the sake of love. Each risk is important to Him and linked to eternal fruit. Through an authentic friendship with the Holy Spirit, we can submit our shaky selves over to the greater purposes of God. And in the meantime, He takes care of our needs and desires.

ENDNOTES

1 Bob Dodson, "Kingdom of Heaven Begins," Acts 242 Study, October 22, 2015. https://acts-242study.com/kingdom-of-heaven-begins/.

"The Yoke of the Kingdom of Heaven," accessed October 14, 2021. http://gatherthepeople.org/Downloads/KINGDOMS_YOKE.pdf.

SMALL GROUP LEADER GUIDE

For those who wish to use this journal curriculum for small group study:

Thank you for your willingness to serve as a small group leader. Those in your group will naturally look to you for leadership to facilitate a discussion where everyone is involved. With a little bit of preparation, you will be ready to serve them in this role. In preparation for your meetings, read the chapter you have designated for the group and go through each question in the study journal.

The most important thing you can do to prepare is to make your personal time with the Lord a priority. Pray for those who are in your group (even if you do not know them) and pray for yourself—that the Lord will open your eyes with His wisdom, discernment, and questions. Since "our struggle is not against flesh and blood, but against the rulers, against the authorities, against the powers of this dark world and against the spiritual forces of evil in the heavenly realms" (Ephesians 6:12), prayer is the key ingredient leading up to your small group interaction.

The journey through *Uncommon Favor: The Intentional Life of a Disciple* will yield impactful encounters with God. The aim as a small group leader is to open the floor for discussion and to extract the treasure from those in your small group. It is a time for them to be vulnerable and to share their responses to what they have been reading as well as some of the important decisions they are making toward becoming disciples of Jesus. Small groups are designed to be like a family that supports and encourages one another and to encourage breakthrough where needed. Listed below are a few tips to help you confidently lead your small group.

- **Start with fun.** Before diving into deeper questions, it's important to first share a bit about yourself and create a safe place that's built on fun. Learn about those in your group, about their families, and ask them why they are reading this book and what they are hoping to get out of their time here.

- **Share your story.** This demonstrates vulnerability and honesty. The Bible says we will overcome the enemy "by the blood of the Lamb and the word of [our] testimony" (Revelation 12:11).

- **Be a good listener.** This is a time for your group to respond to what they have read and what is on their hearts, so your role is to ask questions that are found in the study journal.

- **Don't be afraid of awkward silence.** It can take a bit of time for a small group to feel open to respond to questions. Don't feel like you must fill the empty space by continuing to talk during your meeting time. Embrace awkward silence until someone in your group fills it. Ask open-ended questions, not yes or no questions. Be patient (wait seven seconds before restating the question) and allow them to share.

- **Ask questions.** When it comes to asking questions, start light and gradually go deeper. The goal is to get everyone to express how they are relating to the content.

- **Don't force anything.** Be discerning of where your group is. Calibrate the tempo to suit the flow and pace of your group. Don't worry if you don't get through all the material every week.

- **Pursue quality over quantity.** Small groups are about the quality of conversation rather than quantity. Successful small groups do not revolve around the length of time.

- **Draw your group out.** Don't allow the "talkers" to dominate. Always look for the one who is quiet and draw them out.

- **Keep the conversation focused.** The topic of conversations can quickly get away from you. Don't be afraid to bring it back on track and help guard against anyone getting into their pet doctrines or speculations.

ADDITIONAL RESOURCES

JH Israel website: **jhisrael.com**

JH Ranch website: **jhranch.com**

JH Outback website: **jhoutback.com**

US Israel Education Association website: **usieducation.org**

ALSO AVAILABLE FROM
HEATHER JOHNSTON

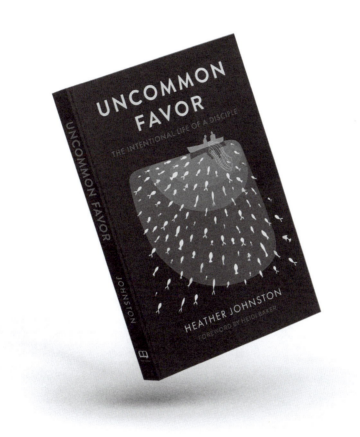

NOW AVAILABLE ON AMAZON
& AT HEATHERJOHNSTON.ORG